ROCK CLASSICS
FOR UKULELE

ISBN 978-1-5400-8236-7

HAL•LEONARD®

Visit Hal Leonard Online at
www.halleonard.com

Contact us:
Hal Leonard
7777 West Bluemound Road
Milwaukee, WI 53213
Email: info@halleonard.com

In Europe, contact:
Hal Leonard Europe Limited
42 Wigmore Street
Marylebone, London, W1U 2RN
Email: info@halleonardeurope.com

In Australia, contact:
Hal Leonard Australia Pty. Ltd.
4 Lentara Court
Cheltenham, Victoria, 3192 Australia
Email: info@halleonard.com.au

Ain't Talkin' 'Bout Love

**Words and Music by Edward Van Halen, Alex Van Halen,
Michael Anthony and David Lee Roth**

Ain't talk - in' 'bout love, just like I told you be - fore, _

To Coda

1. _ yeah, be - fore. 2. You know you're sem - i - good -

2. 3. I been to the edge, _

Verse

_ You know, I lost a lot of friends there, ba - by. I got no time to mess a -

round. So if you want it, got to bleed for it, ba - by.

and there I stood and looked down.

You got to, got to bleed, ba - by.   Mm, you got to, got to

bleed, ba - by.   You got to, got to bleed, ba - by.

D.S. al Coda

Ain't talk - in' 'bout

Coda

Chorus

Ain't talk - in' 'bout   love.

Don't wan - na talk a - bout   love.   Don't need to talk a - bout

love.   Ain't gon - na talk a - bout   love.   Hey! Hey! Hey!

Outro

Play 4 times

Hey! Hey! Hey!   Hey! Hey! Hey!

4

Carry On Wayward Son

Words and Music by Kerry Livgren

Bridge

Car - ry on; you will

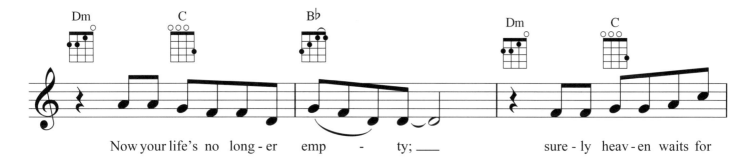

al - ways re - mem - ber. _____ Car - ry on; noth - ing e - quals the splen - dor.

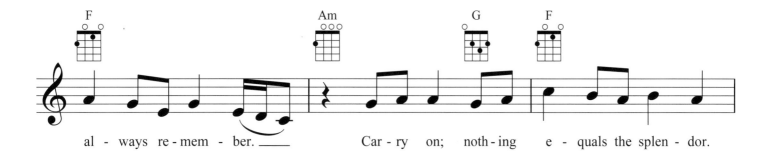

Now your life's no long - er emp - ty; _____ sure - ly heav - en waits for

Chorus

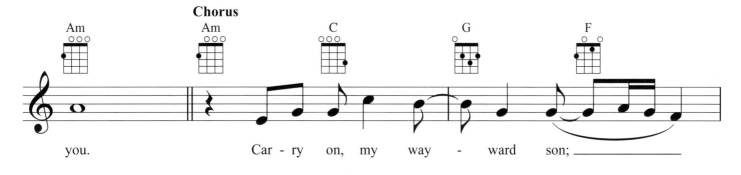

you. Car - ry on, my way - ward son; _____

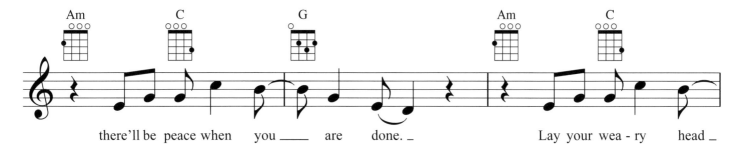

there'll be peace when you ___ are done. _ Lay your wea - ry head _

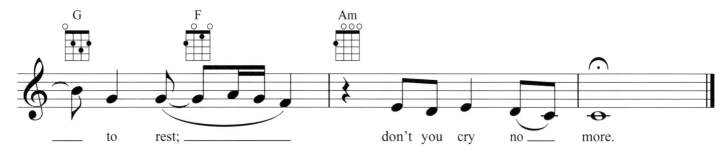

___ to rest; _____ don't you cry no ___ more.

Born to Be Wild

Words and Music by Mars Bonfire

Closer to the Heart

Words and Music by Alex Lifeson, Geddy Lee, Neil Peart and Peter Talbot

(Instrumental)

Don't Stop Believin'

Words and Music by Steve Perry, Neal Schon and Jonathan Cain

Interlude

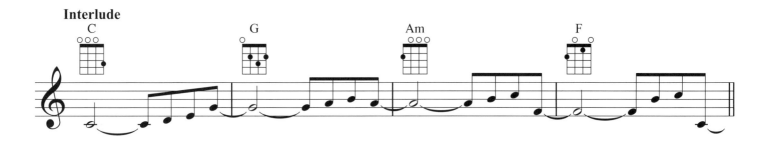

Verse

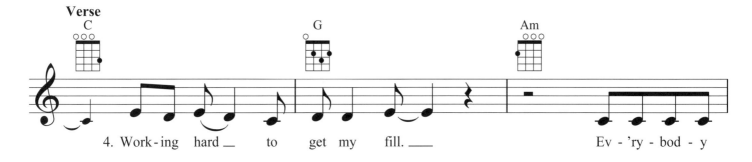

4. Work-ing hard __ to get my fill. __ Ev - 'ry - bod - y

wants a thrill. __ Pay - in' an - y - thing to roll the dice __ just

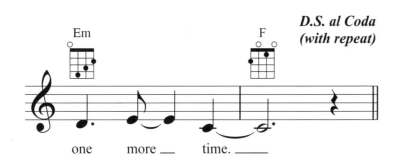

D.S. al Coda (with repeat)

Coda

Outro

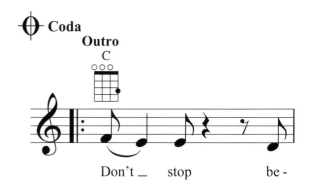

one more __ time. __

Don't __ stop be -

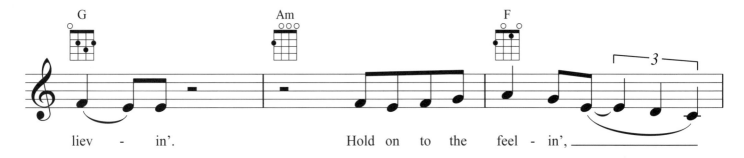

liev - in'. Hold on to the feel - in', __

Repeat and fade

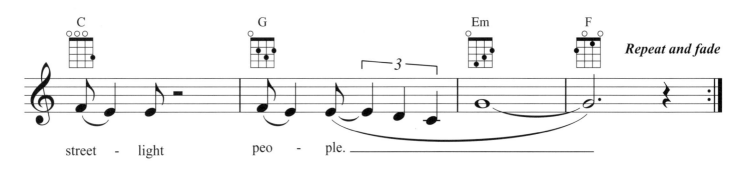

street - light peo - ple. __

14

Come Together

Words and Music by John Lennon and Paul McCartney

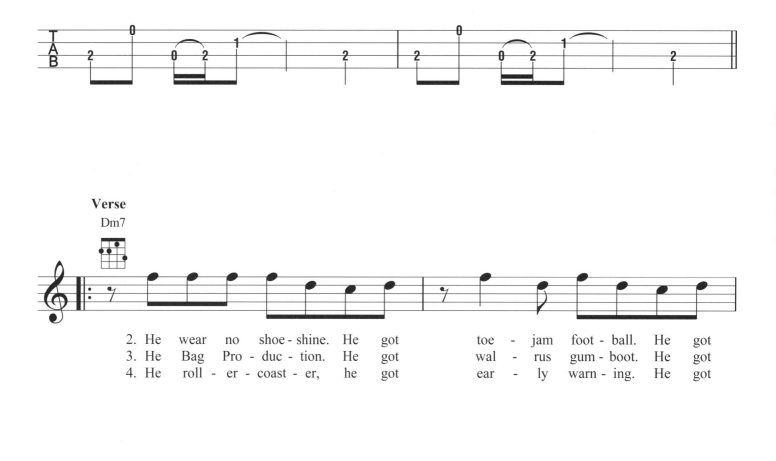

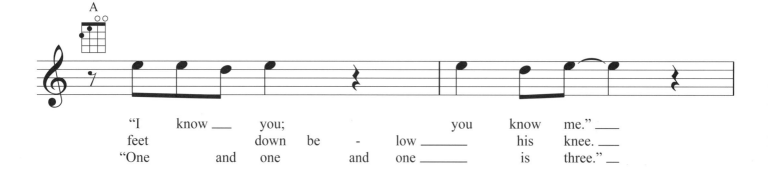

One thing I can tell you is you got to be free. ⟩
Hold you in his arm-chair, you can feel his dis-ease. ⟩ Come to-geth-
Got to be good-look-ing 'cause he so hard to see. ⟩

Chorus

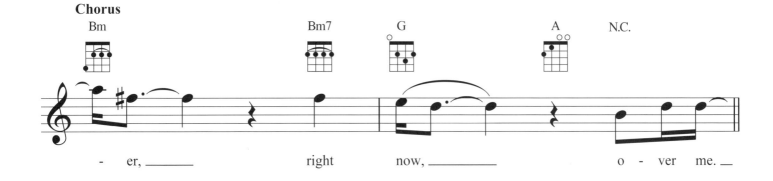

-er, _____ right now, _____ o-ver me. __

Interlude

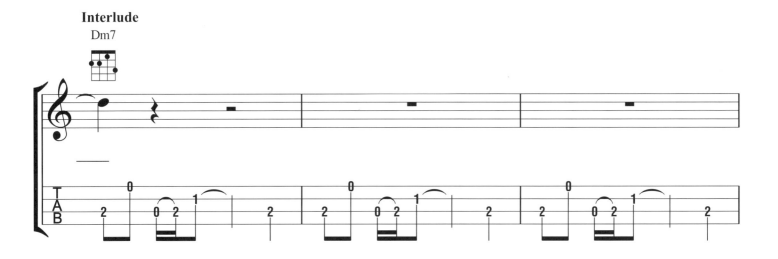

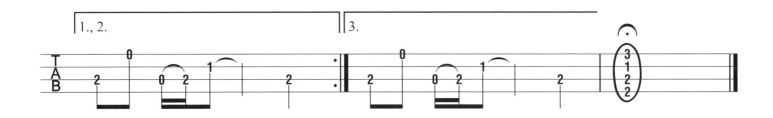

Free Bird

Words and Music by Allen Collins and Ronnie Van Zant

things just could-n't be the same.

'Cause I'm as free ___ as a bird now,

and this bird you can-not change, and this bird you can-not

change, ___ and this bird you can-not change. ___

1.
Lord knows, I can't change. ___

2.
Lord knows, I can't

change. ___ Lord, help me; I can't change.

Go Your Own Way

Words and Music by Lindsey Buckingham

First note

Verse
Moderate Rock

1. Lov - ing you is - n't the right
2. Tell ___ me why ev - 'ry - thing turned ___
3. *Instrumental*

___ thing ___ to do.
___ a - round. How ___ can I ___

___ ev - er change things ___ that ___ I feel? ___
___ shack - ing up's all you wan - na do. ___

How ___ can I ___
Pack - ing up, ___

If ___ I could, ___ may - be I'd give ___ you ___ my world. ___
If ___ I could, ___ ba - by, I'd give ___ you ___ my world. ___

How can I ___ when you won't take ___
O - pen up; ___ ev - 'ry - thing's wait -

Hotel California

Words and Music by Don Henley, Glenn Frey and Don Felder

E7   Am

Such a love - ly place, _ (such a love - ly place,) _ such a love - ly face. _

F   C

Plen - ty of room _ at the Ho - tel Cal - i - for - nia.
They're liv - in' it up ___ at the Ho - tel Cal - i - for - nia.

Dm

An - y time of year, _ (an - y time of year,) _ you can
What a nice sur - prise, _ (what a nice sur - prise,) _ bring your

E7

2nd time, D.C. al Coda

⊕ **Coda**

Am

find it here." _
al - i - bis." __

Additional Lyrics

2. Her mind is Tiffany twisted. She got the Mercedes bends.
She got a lot of pretty, pretty boys that she calls friends.
How they dance in the courtyard; sweet summer sweat.
Some dance to remember, some dance to forget.
So I called up the captain: "Please bring me my wine."
He said, "We haven't had that spirit here since nineteen sixty-nine."
And still those voices are calling from far away;
Wake you up in the middle of the night just to hear them say:

3. Mirrors on the ceiling, the pink champagne on ice,
And she said, "We are all just prisoners here of our own device."
And the master's chambers, they gathered for the feast.
They stab it with their steely knives, but they just can't kill the beast.
Last thing I remember, I was running for the door.
I had to find the passage back to the place I was before.
"Relax," said the night man. "We are programmed to receive.
You can check out any time you like, but you can never leave."

Runnin' Down a Dream

Words and Music by Tom Petty, Jeff Lynne and Mike Campbell

a lit - tle "Run - a - way."   I was fly -
It was al' - ways cold,   no sun - shine. __
I'm pick - in' up   what - ev - er is

- in'.
_____
mine. __

Yeah, run - nin' down a dream __

_____ that nev - er would come to me. _____ Work -

- in' on a mys - ter - y; _____ go - in' wher - ev - er it leads. __

_____ Run - nin' down a dream. _____

Light My Fire

**Words and Music by John Densmore, Robby Krieger,
Ray Manzarek and Jim Morrison**

Livin' on a Prayer

Words and Music by Jon Bon Jovi, Desmond Child and Richie Sambora

First note

Verse
Moderate Rock

1. Tom - my used to work on the docks. ___ Un - ion's been on strike, he's
2. Tom - my's got his six - string in hock, ___ now he's hold - ing in what he

down on his luck. It's tough, ___ so tough. ___
used make to it talk. So tough, ___ it's tough. ___

___ Gi - na works the din - er all day. ___
___ Gi - na dreams of run - ning a - way. ___

___ Work - ing for her man, she brings home her pay for
___ When she cries ___ in the night, Tom - my whis - pers: Ba - by, it's

love, _____

for love. _____

o - kay,

some - day. _____

Pre-Chorus

She says we've got to ⎱
We've got to ⎰ hold on _____ to what we've got. It

does-n't make a dif-f'rence if we make it or not. We've got each oth - er and

that's a lot for _____ love. ___ We'll give it _____ a shot.

Chorus

Whoa, _____ we're half - way there. _____ Whoa, _____ liv -

- in' on a prayer. __ Take my hand, __ we'll make it, I swear. __

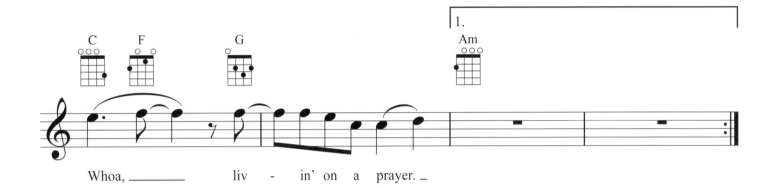

1.

Whoa, _____ liv - in' on a prayer. __

2. **Interlude**

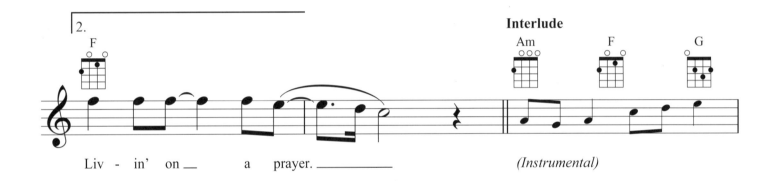

Liv - in' on __ a prayer. _____ *(Instrumental)*

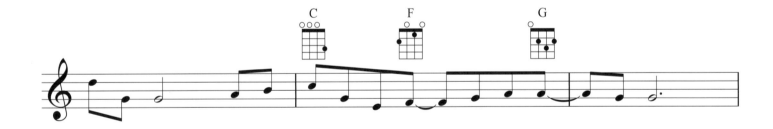

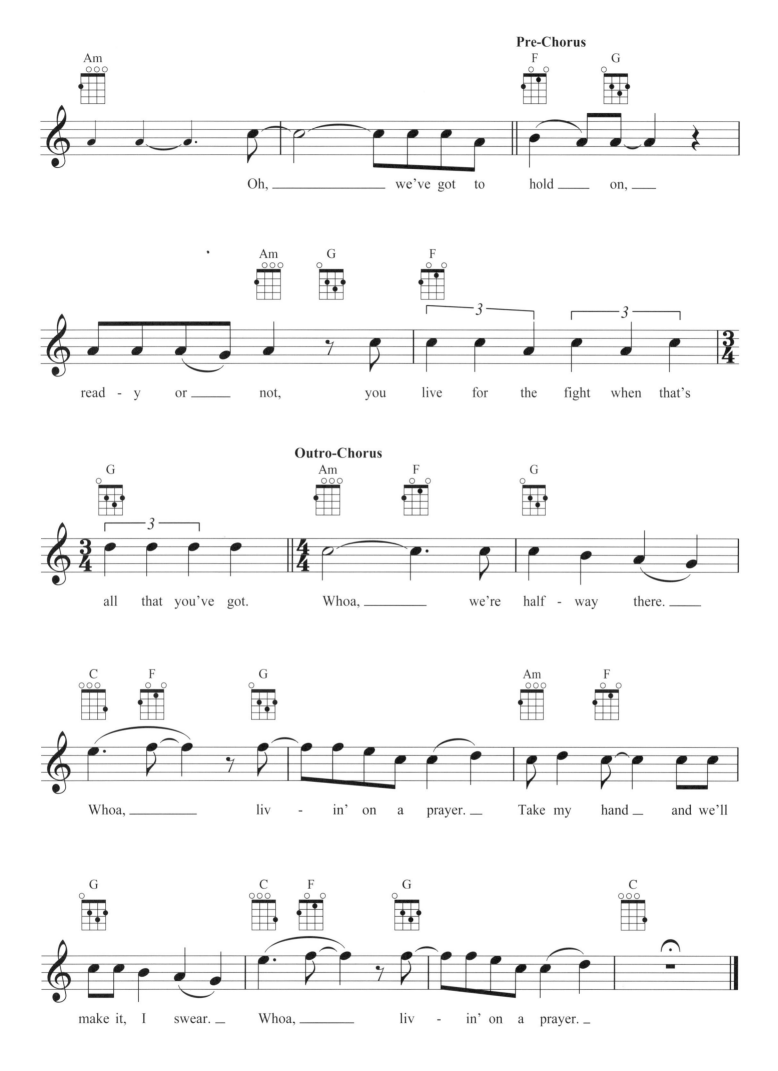

Peace of Mind

Words and Music by Tom Scholz

1. Now, if you're feel-in' kind-a low 'bout the   dues you've been pay-in',
(2.) climb-in'   to   the   top   of   the   com - pa - ny   lad - der,
(3.) bod-y's   got   ad - vice   they   just   keep   on   giv - in',

fu - ture's com - in' much too ___ slow, _____ and you
hope it does - n't take too ___ long. _____ Can't you
does - n't mean too much to me. _____

wan - na run but some - how you just keep on stay - in',
see there'll come a day when it won't mat - ter,
Lots of peo - ple have to make be - lieve they're liv - in';

can't de - cide on which way to go. _____ Yeah, yeah, yeah.
come a day when you'll be gone? _____ Whoa. ___
can't de - cide who they should be. _____ Whoa. ___

Chorus

I un - der - stand ___ a - bout in - de - ci - sion, ___ but I don't care ___ if I

Small Town

Words and Music by John Mellencamp

my par-ents live in the same _____ small town. _____
had my-self a ball in a small _____ town. _____

My job _____ is so small _____ town, pro-vides
Mar-ried an L. A. doll and brought her to this small town, now

lit-tle op-por-tu-ni-ties. _____
she's small town _____ just like _____ me. _____

Bridge

No, I can-not for-get _____ where it is _____ that I _____ come from, I

can-not for-get the peo-ple who love _____ me. Yeah, I can be my-self _____ here in

this small town, _____ and peo-ple let _____ me be _____ just what I want to be.

Verse

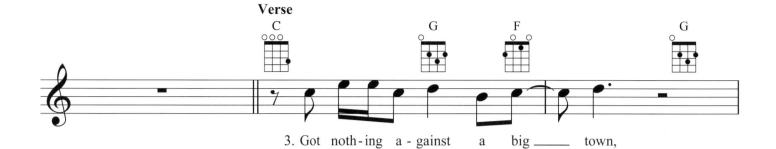

3. Got noth-ing a-gainst a big ___ town,

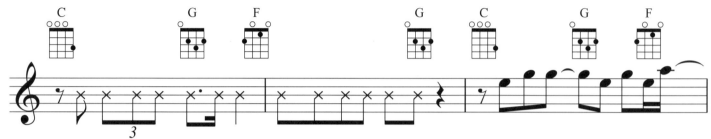

still hay-seed e-nough to say, "Look who's in the big town." But my bed ___ is in a small ___

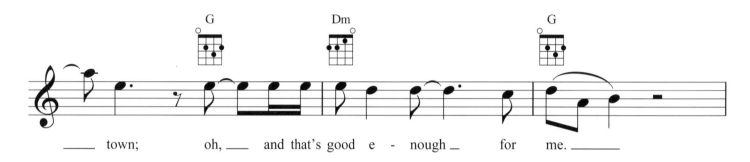

___ town; oh, ___ and that's good e - nough _ for me. ___

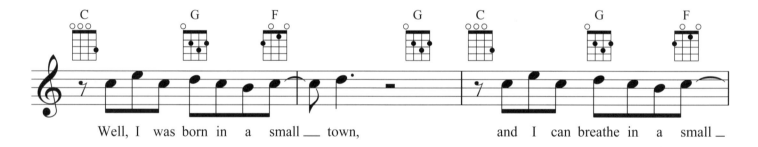

Well, I was born in a small ___ town, and I can breathe in a small ___

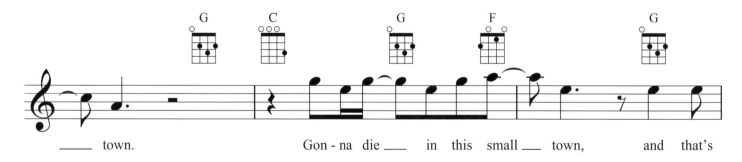

___ town. Gon - na die ___ in this small ___ town, and that's

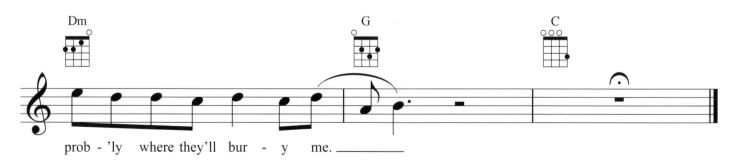

prob - 'ly where they'll bur - y me. ___

Sweet Emotion

Words and Music by Steven Tyler and Tom Hamilton

First note

Chorus
Moderately

Sweet _____ e - mo - tion.

Sweet _____ e - mo - tion. 1. You

Verse

talk a - bout things and no - bod - y cares. __ You're
(2.) sweet - talk - in' ma - ma with a face like a gent __ said my

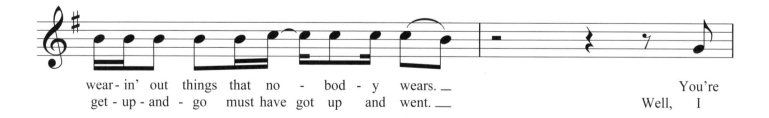

wear - in' out things that no - bod - y wears. __ You're
get - up - and - go must have got up and went. __ Well, I

dad - dy said I took you just a lit - tle too far. You're
take you back - stage, you can drink from my glass. I'm

tell - in' her things but your girl - friend lied; you
talk - in' 'bout some - thin' you can sure un - der - stand, 'cause a

can't catch me 'cause the rab - bit done died.
month on the road and I'll be eat - in' from your hand.

Chorus

G   C   G

Sweet _____ e - mo - tion.

C   G

Sweet _____ e - mo - tion.

Smoke on the Water

Words and Music by Ritchie Blackmore, Ian Gillan,
Roger Glover, Jon Lord and Ian Paice

Somebody to Love

Words and Music by Darby Slick

need some-bod-y to love? ___ Would-n't you love some-bod-y to love? _

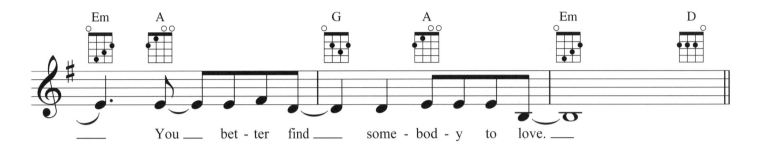

___ You ___ bet-ter find ___ some-bod-y to love. ___

Interlude

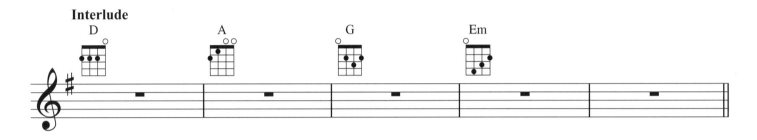

Verse

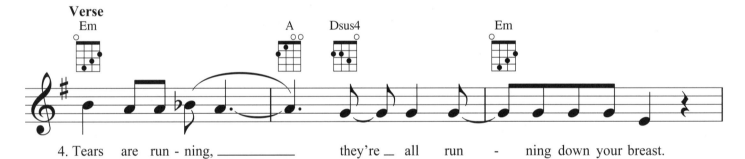

4. Tears are run-ning, _____ they're _ all run - ning down your breast.

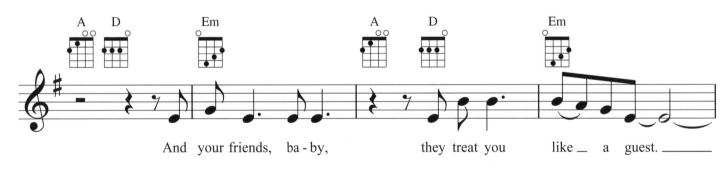

And your friends, ba-by, they treat you like _ a guest. ___

⊕ Coda

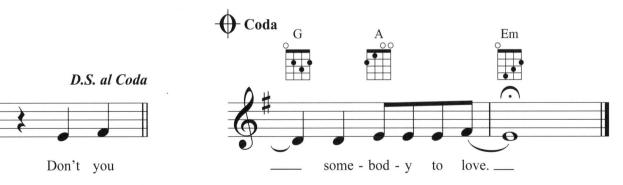

D.S. al Coda

___ Don't you

___ some-bod-y to love. ___

Won't Get Fooled Again

Words and Music by Peter Townshend

cide   and   a   shot - gun   sings   the   song. ____
ban - ners, they   are   flown ____   in   the   last   war. ____
beards have all   grown long - er   o   -   ver - night. ____

I'll tip   my   hat   to   the   new   con - sti - tu - tion,

take   a   bow ___   for   the   new   rev - o - lu - tion,   smile and   grin ___   at   the

change   all   a - round,   pick   up   my   gui - tar   and   play, ____

just   like   yes - ter - day. ____   Then I'll   get   on   my   knees   and

pray   we

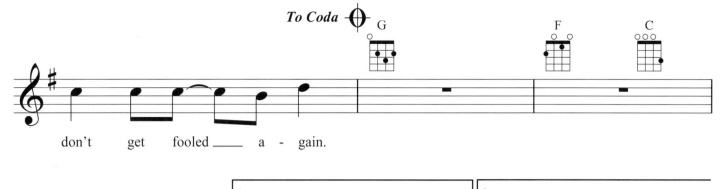

don't get fooled ____ a - gain.

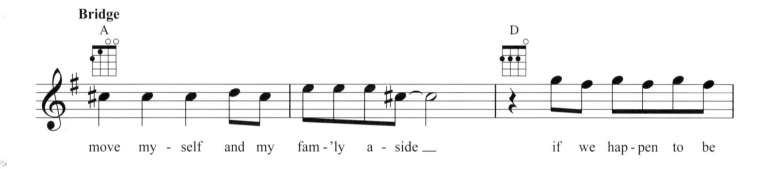

2. I'll   I'll

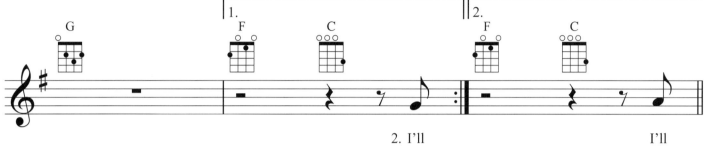

Bridge

move my - self and my fam - 'ly a - side ____ if we hap - pen to be

left half a - live.   I'll get all my pa - pers and smile ____ at the sky, though I

Interlude

know that the hyp - no - tized nev - er lie.

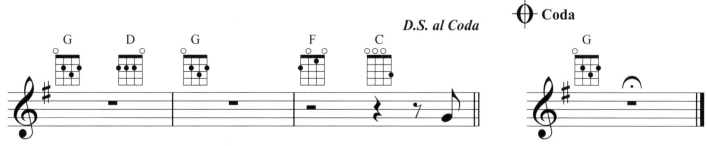

D.S. al Coda   **Coda**

3. There's

Take the Money and Run

Words and Music by Steve Miller

1. This here's a sto-ry 'bout Bil-ly Joe ___ and Bob - by Sue, ___
2. Bil - ly Mack is a de-tec - tive down ___ in Tex - as;

two young lov - ers ___ with ___ noth - in' bet - ter to ___ do ___
you know, he knows ___ just ex - act - ly what ___ the ___ facts is.

than sit a - round the house, get high and watch ___ the tube. ___
He ain't gon - na let those two es - cape ___ jus - tice;

And here's what hap - pened when they de - cid - ed to cut ___ loose:
he makes his liv - ing off of the peo - ple's tax - es.

They head - ed down ___ to ___ old El Pa - so;
Bob - by Sue, ___ oh, ___ she slipped a - way;

that's where they ran ___ in - to a great big has - sle.
Bil - ly Joe ___ caught up to her the ver - y next ___ day.

Bil - ly Joe ___ shot a man while rob - bing his cas - tle;
They got the mon - ey, hey, they got a - way;

Bob - by Sue ___ took the mon - ey and run.
they head - ed down South and they're still run - ning to - day, ___ sing - ing:

𝄋 Chorus

Go on, ___ take the mon - ey and run. Go on, ___ take the mon - ey and

run. Go on, ___ take the mon - ey and run.

1.
2. *D.S. and fade*

Go on, ___ take the mon-ey and run.

Up on Cripple Creek

Words and Music by Robbie Robertson

1. When I get off ___ of this moun-tain, ya know where I wan-na go?

2.–5. *See additional lyrics*

Straight down ___ the Mis - sis-sip-pi Riv-er to the Gulf of Mex - i - co

to Lake Charles, Lou' - si - an - a; lit-tle Bes - sie, girl I once knew.

And she told ___ me just to come on by ___ if there's an-y-thing that she could do.

Additional Lyrics

2. Good luck had just stung me; to the racetrack I did go.
   She bet on one horse to win and I bet on another to show.
   The odds were in my favor; I had 'em five to one.
   When that nag to win came around the track, sure enough we had won.

3. I took up all of my winnings and I gave my little Bessie half.
   She tore it up and threw it in my face just for a laugh.
   Now, there's one thing in the whole wide world I sure would like to see:
   That's when the little love of mine dips her doughnut in my tea.

4. Now, me and my mate were back at the shack; we had Spike Jones on the box.
   She said, "I can't take the way he sings, but I love to hear him talk,"
   Now, that just gave my heart a throb to the bottom of my feet,
   And I swore as I took another pull, my Bessie can't be beat.

5. There's a flood out in California, and up north it's freezing cold,
   And this living off the road is getting pretty old.
   So I guess I'll call up my big mama, tell her I'll be rolling in.
   But you know, deep down, I'm kind of tempted to go and see my Bessie again.

We Are the Champions

Words and Music by Freddie Mercury

The Best Songs Ever

70 songs have now been arranged for ukulele. Includes: Always • Bohemian Rhapsody • Memory • My Favorite Things • Over the Rainbow • Piano Man • What a Wonderful World • Yesterday • You Raise Me Up • and more.

00282413 . . . . $17.99

Disney Hits for Ukulele

Play 23 of your favorite Disney songs on your ukulele. Includes: The Bare Necessities • Cruella De Vil • Do You Want to Build a Snowman? • Kiss the Girl • Lava • Let It Go • Once upon a Dream • A Whole New World • and more.

00151250 . . . . $14.99

Top Hits of 2019

Strum your favorite songs of 2019 on the uke. Includes: Bad Guy (Billie Eilish) • I Don't Care (Ed Sheeran & Justin Bieber) • ME! (Taylor Swift) • Old Town Road (Remix) (Lil Nas X feat. Billy Ray Cyrus) • Senorita (Shawn Mendes & Camila Cabello) • Someone You Loved (Lewis Capaldi) • and more.

00302274 . . . . $14.99

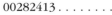

Campfire Songs for Ukulele

30 favorites to sing as you roast marshmallows and strum your uke around the campfire. Includes: God Bless the U.S.A. • Hallelujah • The House of the Rising Sun • I Walk the Line • Puff the Magic Dragon • Wagon Wheel • You Are My Sunshine • and more.

00129170 . . . . $14.99

First 50 Songs You Should Play on Ukulele

An amazing collection of 50 accessible, must-know favorites: Edelweiss • Hey, Soul Sister • I Walk the Line • I'm Yours • Imagine • Over the Rainbow • Peaceful Easy Feeling • The Rainbow Connection • Riptide • and many more.

00149250 . . . . $14.99

The Ukulele 3 Chord Songbook

If you know three chords, you can play these 50 great hits! Songs include: Bad Moon Rising • A Boy Named Sue • King of the Road • Leaving on a Jet Plane • Shelter from the Storm • Time for Me to Fly • Twist and Shout • and many more.

00141143 . . . . $16.99

The Daily Ukulele

compiled and arranged by Liz and Jim Beloff
Strum a different song everyday with easy arrangements of 365 of your favorite songs in one big songbook! Includes favorites by the Beatles, Beach Boys, and Bob Dylan, folk songs, pop songs, kids' songs, Christmas carols, and Broadway and Hollywood tunes, all with a spiral binding for ease of use.

00240356 . . . . $39.99

The Ukulele 4 Chord Songbook

With just 4 chords, you can play 50 hot songs on your ukulele! Songs include: Brown Eyed Girl • Do Wah Diddy Diddy • Hey Ya! • Ho Hey • Jessie's Girl • Let It Be • One Love • Stand by Me • Toes • With or Without You • and many more.

00142050 . . . . $16.99

The Ultimate Ukulele Fake Book

Uke enthusiasts will love this giant, spiral-bound collection of over 400 songs for uke! Includes: Crazy • Dancing Queen • Downtown • Fields of Gold • Happy • Hey Jude • 7 Years • Summertime • Thinking Out Loud • Thriller • Wagon Wheel • and more.

00175500 . . . . $45.00

The Daily Ukulele – Leap Year Edition

366 More Songs for Better Living
compiled and arranged by Liz and Jim Beloff
An amazing second volume with 366 MORE songs for you to master each day of a leap year! Includes: Ain't No Sunshine • Calendar Girl • I Got You Babe • Lean on Me • Moondance • and many, many more.

00240681 . . . . $39.99

Simple Songs for Ukulele

50 favorites for standard G-C-E-A ukulele tuning, including: All Along the Watchtower • Can't Help Falling in Love • Don't Worry, Be Happy • Ho Hey • I'm Yours • King of the Road • Sweet Home Alabama • You Are My Sunshine • and more.

00156815 . . . . $14.99

Ukulele – The Most Requested Songs

Strum & Sing Series
Cherry Lane Music
Nearly 50 favorites all expertly arranged for ukulele! Includes: Bubbly • Build Me Up, Buttercup • Cecilia • Georgia on My Mind • Kokomo • L-O-V-E • Your Body Is a Wonderland • and dozens more.

02501453 . . . . $14.99